Mon and the Log

By Sally Cowan

It was hot.

Mon's mum had a nap.

Mon ran to the mud pit.

He met Kip.

Kip sat on a log.

"Look at the bugs
in the mud!" said Kip.

"I can get bugs," said Mon.

Mon dug and dug.

He got wet.

But he did not get the bugs.

The bugs hid in the mud.

"Look! Ants!" said Kip.

"I can get ants!" said Mon.

The ants ran on the log.

Mon hit at the ants.

But the log got up!

"Kip! It is **not** a log!"
said Mon.

Mon ran up to Mum.

He sat on Mum's lap.

CHECKING FOR MEANING

1. What does Mon think the crocodile is? *(Literal)*

2. How does Mon try to catch the bugs in the mud? *(Literal)*

3. How do you think the crocodile was feeling when Mon and Kip tried to get the ants crawling on it? *(Inferential)*

EXTENDING VOCABULARY

ran	The word *ran* means moved faster than a walk. What other words could have been used instead of *ran* in *Mon ran up to Mum*?
hid	What sounds are in the word *hid*? What other words do you know that end in *–id*?
Mum's	Look at the word *Mum's*. What is the base of this word? Why has an apostrophe and an *s* been added to the end of *Mum*?

MOVING BEYOND THE TEXT

1. Did you like the ending of the story? Why or why not?

2. How do you think monkeys spend their time during the day?

3. Would you rather be a monkey, an ant or a crocodile? Why?

4. What might Mon have learned during this story?

SPEED SOUNDS

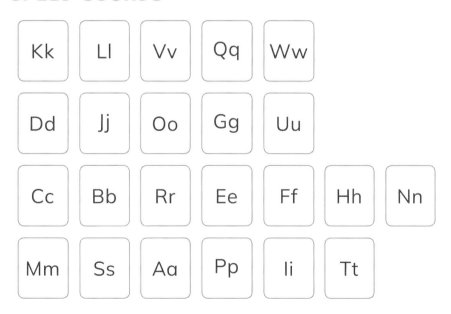

Kk	Ll	Vv	Qq	Ww
Dd	Jj	Oo	Gg	Uu

Cc	Bb	Rr	Ee	Ff	Hh	Nn

Mm	Ss	Aa	Pp	Ii	Tt

PRACTICE WORDS

log

Kip

lap

wet